W9-BTH-403

NOT HEARD ON THE STREET

An Irreverent Dictionary of Wall Street

MAURICE JOY

PROBUS PUBLISHING COMPANY
Chicago, Illinois

This publication is designed to provide accurate and authoritative information in regard to the subject matter covered. It is sold with the understanding that the publisher is not engaged in rendering legal, accounting or other professional service. If legal advice or other expert assistance is required, the services of a competent professional person should be sought.

FROM A DECLARATION OF PRINCIPLES JOINTLY ADOPTED BY A COMMITTEE OF THE AMERICAN BAR ASSOCIATION AND A COMMITTEE OF PUBLISHERS.

Library of Congress Cataloging in Publication Data Available Upon Request

ISBN 0-917253-40-x

Library of Congress Catalog Card No.

Printed in the United States of America

1 2 3 4 5 6 7 8 9 0

One horse-laugh is worth
ten thousand syllogisms.

H. L. Mencken

Introduction

Will Rogers once said he never met a man he didn't like. But then, he never knew any of my financial advisors. Maybe you know someone else Will never met. If you've ever had any dealings with Wall Street, you've probably met some bonds and stocks you didn't like. On the other hand, if all your financial transactions have been happy ones . . . you just haven't been in the market long enough. Stick around, you'll get yours!

This book was written for all those who have been around long enough to have gotten theirs. Since that doesn't take long, the book is, of course, for almost everyone. Never mind that there have been victories in between the defeats. Everyone knows that victories are fleeting and defeats linger.

If it's true that laughing at a problem diminishes it, this book is intended to shrink your problems, however few, to a manageable size.

The impetus for the book comes from two sources: (1) a feverish mind, and (2) the firmly held conviction that all is not as it seems. Little should be said about the first item—we each have our minor faults. It's the second item that's crucial. It is, in fact, important to recognize that point in all its various forms. It's not enough, for example, to know that you shouldn't believe everything you read, because radio, tv and other friends are working on us also.

Once you take to heart this simple truth—and depending on how feverish your mind is—alternative interpretations of everything soon start appearing. Three short examples will suffice:

Talk Is Cheap

My luncheon companion lays it on thick. He made enough on his stocks this month to retire to Sun City. More likely, he made enough to offset—but only just—his losses in previous months. Certainly, he didn't make enough to insist on paying the lunch tab.

So Are Sales Pitches

My broker calls me up and offers 10,000 shares of Amalgamated Disunited, Inc. It is, she assures me, the best new issue since Genentech. Now that *is* good news. I remember the Genentech deal very well. It was so good I couldn't get any of it. What my broker is now telling me is that I've become an important person. And if you believe that one, there's a really neat bridge I'd like to sell you.

And So are Explanations

Pick up any copy of any newspaper or magazine that follows the stock market regularly and you'll see it: *the* definitive explanation. The market went down because . . . . Or, the market went up because . . . . You may think it's hard to pin down the real reason stock prices change. Actually, it is. But not if you've got a grab bag of explanations that can be rummaged through. One of them ought to work. And, I suppose that's true. Nobody can be wrong all the time.

The two immutable truths of Finance are that investors are motivated by greed and fear. I agree, but only partially; there is a third motivator: loathing. I maintain you will never understand fully what Wall Street is all about if all you have to rely on is greed and fear. You also need loathing. Besides, loathing is funnier.

Of course, humor of this kind can be distinctly unhumorous to those on the wrong side of the joke. So, let me make my amends up front to all parties slighted by my misguided irreverence: Nothing personal intended, dear hearts; I still like you all.

You don't believe me?

I'll bet you'd never have said that to Will Rogers.

Maurice Joy

What Have You Heard On The Street?

If you have a definition of "Wall Street-ese" that's unique, oblique and worthy of a few modest laughs then we'd like to hear from you. Just fill out this card with your definition(s), name and address.

If your definition is accepted by our editors (a committee of curmudgeonly pundits) it will be included in the next edition of *Not Heard on the Street* with your name cited as its author.

Definition
_____
_____
_____

Name
_____
Address
_____
City   State   Zip

Definitions will be published solely at the discretion of Probus Publishing Company. No royalties or payments of any kind will be made for the definitions submitted.

Address submissions to:

Probus Publishing Company
118 N. Clinton
Suite 305
Chicago, IL 60606

Accelerated depreciation. What your stocks' prices suffer from.

Account executive. A fancy name for an ex-car salesman.

Accountant. The person who records all the mistakes management makes.

Accounting policy. A collection of choices—all consistent with generally accepted accounting principles, of course—designed to make current earnings look good irrespective of what's really going on.

Accrued interest. The thing you always owe the other person in a bond sale.

Accumulation area. A technical analyst's explanation of why your stock's price is stuck. (Well, no one else knows the reason either.)

Active market. How your broker views your account.

Advance/decline. What your shorts and longs do, respectively.

Advance refunding. Where a company admits its mistake early.

Advisory service. Having Ann Landers pick your stocks.

Agencies. Being rolled by bureaucrats in the bond market.

Alligator spread. Losing your Izod in the options market.

American Depository Receipt. A way to lose U.S. dollars in foreign stocks.

Amortize. Taken from the Latin, meaning a prolonged death, but on schedule.

Analyst. Either a recently graduated MBA who doesn't understand the market or a Wall Street veteran who doesn't understand the market.

Annual report. An explanation of why the past twelve months were so disastrous along with a prediction of cheery times ahead.

Arbitrage. Buying and selling identical assets at different prices to lock in a loss.

Arrearage. What preferred stockholders fall on when their dividends are omitted.

Asian CD. Having your money shanghaied in Hong Kong.

Ask price. The price at which no one will buy your stock.

Assets. What management sits on.

At the market. Abbreviation for the phrase "at the mercy of the market."

Auditors' report. Professional verification that your company's results are indeed as bad as they seem.

Authorized shares. A dark hint that there may be some unauthorized shares out there also.

Automatic dividend reinvestment plan. A way to continuously deepen your losses without a lot of administrative hassle.

Average. What you can't beat in the stock market.

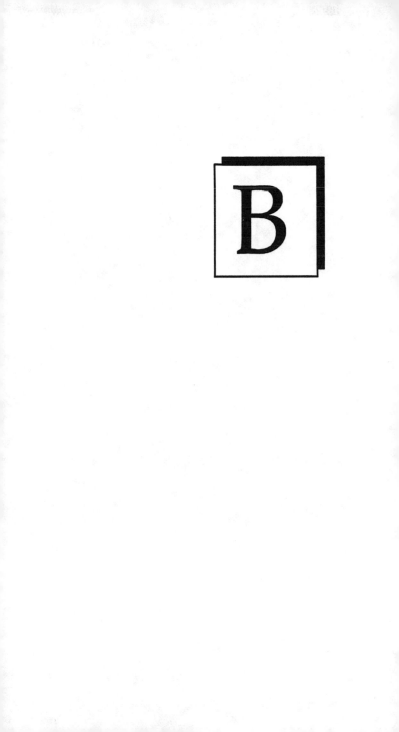

Baby bond.   A debt security designed to help you lose money in smaller-than-standard increments.

Back office.   Where the folks who mangle your security bookkeeping transactions work.

Balanced fund.   Mutual funds that hold both poor growth stocks and poor income securities.

Balance of trade.   A number designed specifically to show how much better off Japan is than we are.

Balance sheet.   The accountants' insistence that assets equal liabilities plus equities, even when the assets aren't worth anything.

Balloon payment.   A debt obligation about to go pop.

Bankers' acceptance.   Attractive investments whose minimum denomination requirements preclude you from buying them.

Bankers' year. Finding out that there are only 360 days in the year *and* that that means—only incidentally, of course—the bank makes a few more dollars in interest off you.

Bankruptcy. A disastrous event that rarely occurs, except for the few companies you invest in.

Bar chart. A visual representation of how your stocks have decreased in value over time.

Basis point. A way to convey how much you lost in more detailed terms than mere percentages.

Bear market. What a stock goes through right after you buy it.

Bearer bond. A safari term used to remind us that the capital market is a jungle.

Best efforts. Finding out that talk is cheap.

Beta. A college fraternity that, in some incomprehensible way, is concerned with risk.

Bid price. The price at which no one will sell you stock.

Big Board. The most prestigious group of mediocre investments in the world.

Bills. Government securities so unattractive they always trade at a discount.

Black Thursday. Any Thursday in the stock market.

Blanket recommendation. Having Linus as your investment advisor.

Block sale. A sure sign the neighborhood's going downhill.

Blue chip. A stock whose reputation far exceeds its performance.

Blue sky laws. Cold comfort when flying in a plane in which the pilot is a crook.

Board room. Where the high-level office parties are held.

Boiler room. Where your broker calls you from.

Book value. What your stock would be worth if management had even a shred of competence.

Bonds.   Things that tie up your portfolio.

Bottom line.   Where the red ink goes.

Breadth of market.   Widespread mayhem.

Break-even.   Something you'll never see.

Breakout.   A prison term used to lend excitement to a five-point rally in the Dow.

Bridge loan.   Borrowing money to erect a flimsy structure over a murderous ravine.

Broker.   A person licensed to help you go broke.

Bucket shop.   A basketball term that means you've been slam-dunked by your broker.

Budget constraint.   What you should always live within, even if you must borrow to do so.

Bull.   What your investment advisor tells you.

Bull market.   Where the supply of and the demand for investment advisors meet.

Business cycle.   A vehicle with no handlebars that moves in unpredictable ways.

Businessman's risk.   Your broker's definition of a tolerable risk, loosely stated as no more than an 80 percent chance of losing everything you own.

Butterfly spread.   Being chloroformed and tacked to the wall in the options market.

Buy and hold.   An investment strategy used exclusively during bear markets.

Buy stop order.   A way to pick up a stock at its very highest price.

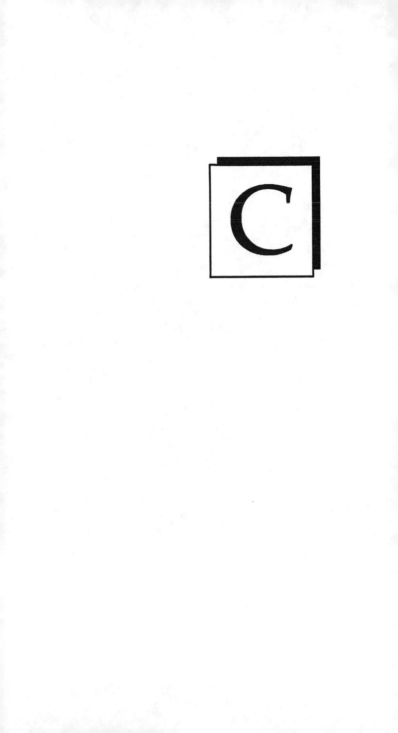

Call option. Something you write just before the stock price goes up.

Call feature. A device that allows the only good bond you ever owned to be taken away from you.

Call protection. Something that exists only in the mind of the naive investor.

Capital asset pricing model (CAPM). A fancy theory dreamed up by college professors that tells you—always after the fact—why you lost a bundle in the market.

Capital in excess of par. An obscure accounting term that shows how much you overpaid for your stock.

Capital gains. What you need to balance off your capital losses.

Capital market. A market where you lose your capital.

Capitalization rate. The speed at which you lose your capital.

Cash equivalents. Where you trade good cash for bad substitutes.

Cash flow. That thing that always goes out and never comes in.

Certificate of deposit. Proof that you own a bad investment.

Charting. The triumph of form over substance.

Checking the market. Updating the bad news.

Churning. What your broker does with your account on an otherwise slow day; or, what your stomach does when you review your annual commission expenses.

Client update. Finding out how the customer would prefer to lose money this year.

Close-end fund. A mutual fund not worth the securities it owns.

Collateral. What the lenders insist upon before they'll loan you the money to invest in that ironclad, no-lose, guaranteed win, lead-pipe cinch investment.

Commercial paper. The stuff you bought from Penn Central in 1970.

Commercial bank. A depository institution that pays you less than the prevailing market interest rate.

Commingled funds. An attempt to disguise how badly things are going for any one account.

Commission. What your broker maximizes.

Commodity market. A place where you can learn high finance and lose the farm at the same time.

Common stock. A dull title for a risky investment.

Compounding. How your losses grow over time.

Confidence index. An infinitely large number that equals the difference between your broker's expectations and those of sane people.

Conglomerate. A geology term for companies whose management team is right out of the stone age.

Consolidated statements. A way to disguise how badly the subsidiaries and parent company are doing individually.

Consumer price index. A number that goes up twice as much as your stocks' prices go down.

Consumer stocks. Stocks that eat up money put into them.

Contrarian. A broker who sells short what you told her to buy.

Conventional wisdom. Consoling yourself with the fact everyone else was wrong too.

Conversion price. The price at which you undergo a stunning religious experience.

Conversion ratio. How many stunning religious experiences you can stand.

Convertible bond. A bond with no top . . . or seat belt.

Corner. A place where you get mugged.

Council of Economic Advisors. A group of economists whose predictions haven't become widely enough known yet to discredit them fully, but who are working on it.

Coupon bond. Where your bonds are only worth a hamburger, fries and medium Pepsi.

Covenant. A religious term describing what your company just violated on its loan agreements.

Cover. Being short-sheeted in the foreign exchange market.

Covered call writing. A hedge against capital gains.

Credit analysis. What you assumed your advisor did before recommending those WPPS bonds.

Cum rights. Using Latin to say that your bad shares allow you the first chance to buy more of the same.

Cumulative preferred. A provision designed to protect preferred stockholders, which ought to make you suspicious right from the start.

Curb. A cute name for a place to lose money other than the NYSE.

Current assets. What your company just ran out of.

Current liabilities. Your broker, your banker, your financial advisor and all your spouse's family.

Current yield. What your bond is giving up now.

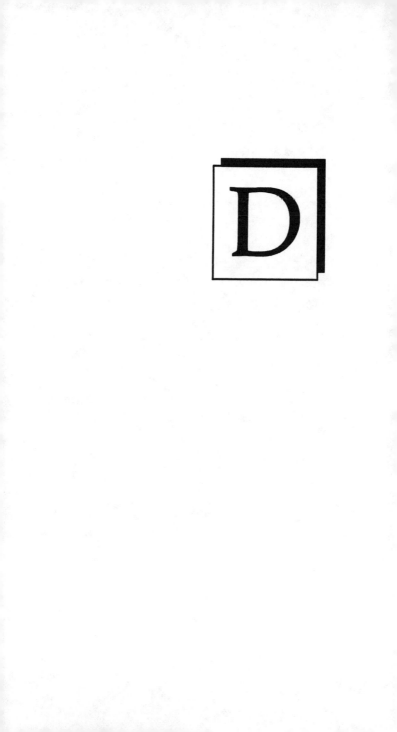

Dealer. The person who controls the cards.

Debenture. An unsecured seat.

Debt. Past tense of "die."

Deep discount bond. What a bond becomes right after you buy it.

Deep in the money. Invariably, the other person's position.

Deep out of the money. Your position.

Default risk. What every one of your bonds is loaded with.

Defeasance. A bad Amos and Andy joke applied to accounting.

Deficit. Business as usual in Congress.

Deflation. What will happen after you've carefully arranged your affairs to cope with inflation.

Depletion. What your portfolio experiences on an average day.

Depreciation. What your portfolio experiences on a good day.

Depression. What you get when you read the daily stock quotations.

Digits deleted. Richard Nixon's financial transactions put on White House tapes.

Dilution. The least destructive thing that happened to your company's earnings per share all year.

Direct placement. Debt so attractive only the Big Boys get it.

Director. A motion picture title given to someone who overruns the budget.

Disclosure. What will happen to all useless information.

Discount broker. Proof that you get what you pay for.

Discount rate. The speed with which you lose faith in the Fed.

Discretionary account. An arrangement where your broker loses your money without continually getting your approval.

Disintermediation. A loan officer embezzles from a bank.

Diversification. Losing money across a wide range of investments.

Dividend. What your best stock just omitted.

Dividend reinvestment plan. The triumph of hope over experience.

Dollar cost averaging. A formula investing plan for spreading your losses over several time periods.

Dow Jones Industrial Average. A relatively poor performance market index that always does better than your portfolio.

Dow Theory. Proof that superstition and tea-leaf reading still thrive in the Western world.

Downtick. The best thing that happened to your stock all week.

Dual purpose fund. A way to divide up losses between income and capital gains.

Duration. How long your spouse carps about your latest investment.

Dynamic market. A market where you get clobbered hard and often.

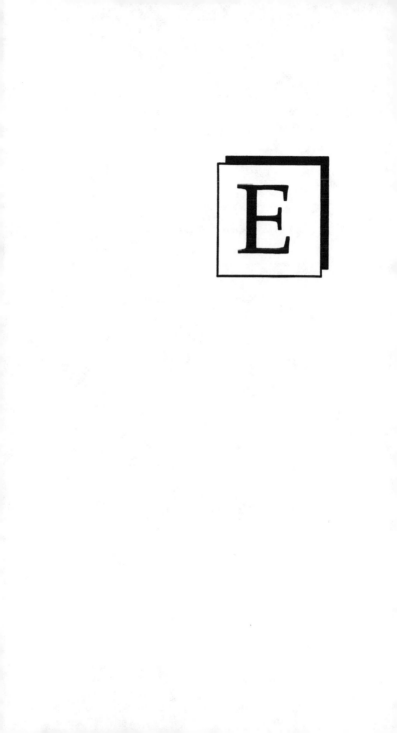

Earnings. A misnomer showing how much your company lost last period.

Earnings per share. The same misnomer put on a per-share basis.

Earnings yield. Your company's profits just surrendered.

Economic forecasts. An attempt to make astrologists look good.

Efficient market hypothesis. A fancy theory that basically says: when the other guy makes money he's either cheating or downright lucky, but that you shouldn't expect to do so well.

End-of-year tax planning. Locking the barn door after the horse has run away.

Energy stocks. Your oil stocks that just ran out of gas.

Equipment trust. Actually, you should never trust anybody or anything on Wall Street, and especially not equipment.

Equity. Something only the other guy gets.

Escheat. Hispanic for being cheated.

Escrow. More vivid Hispanic for being cheated, pluperfect tense.

Eurobonds. A way for you personally to perpetuate the Marshall Plan.

Exchange rate. The terms at which you trade good money for bad.

Execution. What you'd like to do to your broker.

Exercise price. A gymnastics term that relates to dropping a barbell on your foot.

Exercise ratio. How many barbells get dropped on your foot.

Extraordinary item. Dignified accounting definition for a wild financial transaction.

Extraordinary losses. Losses that are nonrecurring only in the sense that the reasons for the losses change from year to year.

Face value. A situation where the most valuable feature of your bond is the picture on the certificate.

Factoring. An algebra term applied to borrowing that reinforces why you never liked algebra.

Fair market value. Life isn't fair, so who said market value would be any different?

Family of funds. Investing with the Mafia.

Fannie Mae. Taking a spring pratfall in the agencies market.

Fed funds rate. A borrowing rate so good you're not allowed to use it.

Federal budget deficit. A number half as large as your current year's stock losses.

Federal Reserve Board of Governors. The group that always moves the money supply the wrong way at the wrong time.

Fidelity bond. A flagrant misuse of an adjective.

Fiduciary. A relationship of trust that is violated only when the trustees think they can get away with it.

Filter technique. A strategy where either you trade often with a large number of small losses or you trade seldom with big losses.

Financial Accounting Standards Board (FASB). A prestigious group that understands little about accounting and even less about standards.

Financial advisor. To err is human, but to be paid for it is divine.

Financial risk. What your investments share with that good ship, the Titanic.

Fixed charges. A more apt description would be "stuck" charges because no matter which way interest rates move, someone will get stuck.

Flat. How a bond is priced when it blows a tire.

Floating rate debt.   One of several nautical terms used in the debt market—another is sinking fund—to emphasize that we are in constant peril of drowning.

Floor.   The theoretical support level your bonds just fell through.

Flower bonds.   Something only your heirs will see the blooms on.

Forecasts.   What everyone on Wall Street does often and badly.

Foreign exchange.   Gresham's Law in an international setting.

Forward contract.   A way to lock up a foreign exchange loss.

Fourth market.   Being outwitted by a computer.

Freddie Mac.   Two shares of McDonald's sandwiched around one bad mortgage, with no mustard.

Free lunch.   Something that doesn't exist, but everyone keeps looking for anyway.

Full-service broker.   A stock broker who will charge you fully for all services offered, whether you use them or not.

Fundamental analysis. Being wrong about the stock market even though the scenario sounds perfectly believable.

Funded debt.   Long-term trouble.

Fungible.   Something that grows on the north side of trees

Futures market. Wrestling with Darth Vader without the aid of the Force.

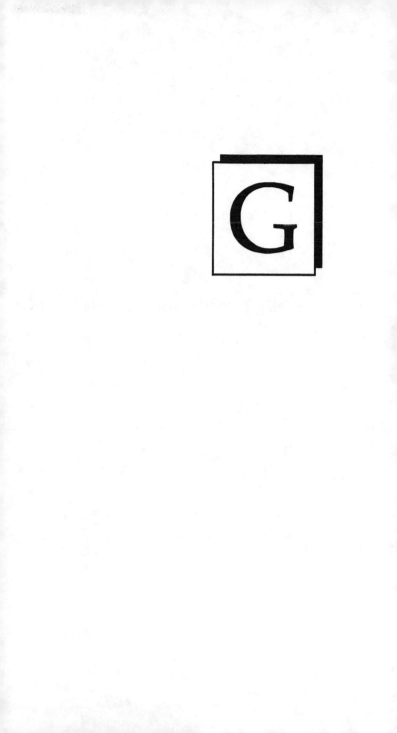

General obligation bonds. An egregious attempt by municipalities to make you believe they stand behind their debt.

Generally accepted accounting principles (GAAP). A set of guidelines that allows the accountants to cook the books any way management wants.

Ginnie Maes. Something you would buy only after a three martini lunch.

Gnomes. Financial version of leprechauns, with evil overtones.

Go-Go fund. A mutual fund twice as safe as your bonds.

Gold bug. Your mother was right, you shouldn't play with insects.

Golden parachute. A World War II movie with the company's top officers cast as the 82d Airborne and the stockholders playing the enemy. Guess who wins?

Good delivery. Something you get only from Pizza Hut.

Good management. A second-rate quarterback running a third-rate team.

Goodwill. A poor substitute for market value.

Government bonds. The safest thing in the market, unless the folks who issue them crank up inflation . . . which they always do.

Great crash. Any Friday in your portfolio.

Green mail. Proof that the meek will not inherent the earth.

Gross National Product (GNP). A phrase coined by an economist with a sense of humor to describe how lean things are at the macro level.

Gross profit. A contradiction of terms.

Growth stock. A stock whose earnings double while, simultaneously, the price drops.

Guaranteed income contract (GIC). Alimony to your ex-spouse.

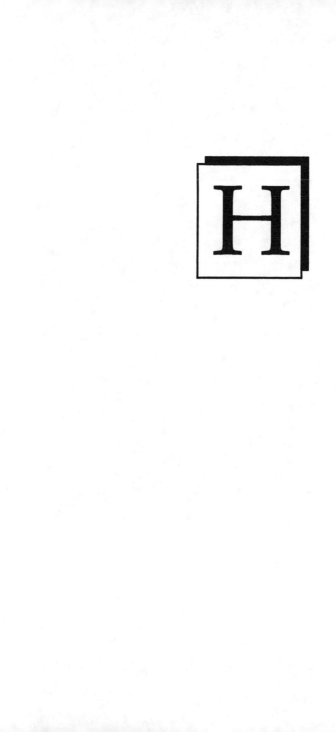

Head and shoulders top. A shampoo used just before you take a bath in the stock market.

Hedging. An action that neutralizes what would otherwise have been a profitable position.

Hemline theory. The financial proof that chasing skirts doesn't pay.

High flyer. The stock you just shorted.

High-grade bonds. One word will suffice: WHOOPS.

High-tech stock. A computer company that, right after you buy its stock, diversifies heavily into double-knits.

Historical cost. A meaningless cost that the accountants keep careful records on.

Holder of record. Guiness identifies you as the world's worst investor.

Holding company. One mediocre company that owns controlling interest in one or more other mediocre companies.

Holocaust. A dull day in the futures market.

I

Immunization. Voluntarily cutting off your leg to avoid getting chicken pox in your bond portfolio.

In-and-out trader. Your broker's idea of a long-term investor.

In the money. An options term that is not descriptive of your performance in the options market.

Income bond. A misleading name for a bond that pays interest only on those rare occasions when the company earns it.

Income fund. A mutual fund that provides high income in return for higher capital losses.

Income statement. A euphoric name for loss statement.

Indenture. Being bound to a bad bond.

Index fund. An easy way to duplicate average market losses.

Inflation. What your investments can't keep up with.

Insiders. Everyone else in the market.

Institutional investor. The folks who stampede out of a stock just after you buy in.

Intangible assets. All those things your company has that aren't worth anything.

Interest. What your bonds just omitted.

Interest coverage. Finding out from the six o'clock news what your bonds just omitted.

Interest rate. There are actually two: the absurdly low one you receive and the preposterously high one you pay.

Interest rate risk. Watching your bonds travel through the Bermuda Triangle.

Interest sensitive stock. Where your stock goes down regardless which way interest rates move.

International diversification. Losing money in more than one country.

Intrinsic value. Another poor substitute for market value.

Inventory. Tallying up the long list of bad investments you own.

Investment. A speculation before it goes bad.

Investment banker. A market professional who helps your broker find bad stocks and bonds to pass along to you.

Investment grade. In your portfolio, mostly Ds and Fs.

Investment philosophy. What your broker stresses when things are going bad.

Investment tax credit. A tax break Congress has authorized, signifying they think your investments are so bad you need it.

Investor. A euphemism for someone who's locked into a big loss.

IRA. A way to lose your money without sending it to Northern Ireland.

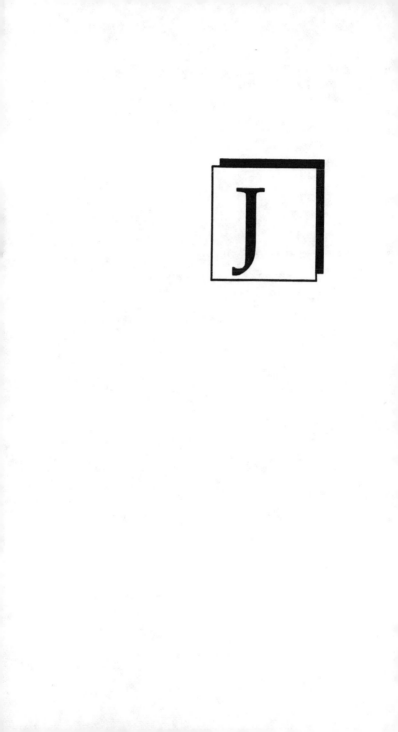

J

Junior capital.   Betting that a boy can do a man's job.

Junk bonds.   Bonds with significantly better quality than those you own.

Justified price.   What the price of your stock would be if the market were as naive as you.

Keogh plan. A way to sock away tax losses for retirement.

Kicker. As every football fan knows, there are two kinds of kickers: punters and field goal specialists. A kicker in the financial sense of the word is always a punter.

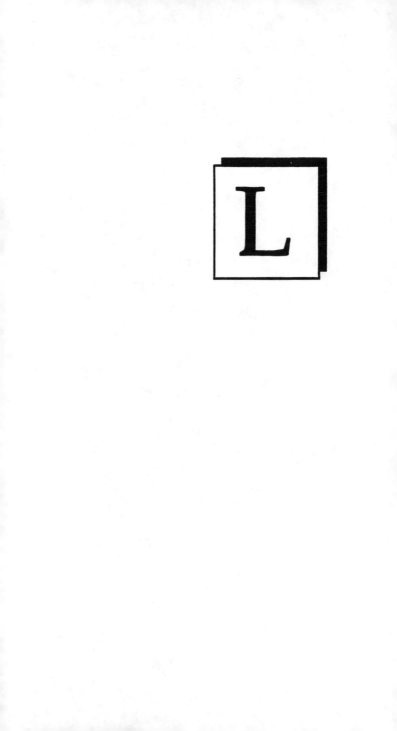

Laddering.   Guaranteeing that your bond portfolio will never do better than average.

Laffer curve.   Proof that economics is not a dismal science, nor, for that matter, any kind of science.

Leading indicators.   Economic harbingers that turn favorable just before your stocks nosedive.

Lease obligations.   Liabilities so important management wants to stick them in the footnotes of the annual report.

Lender.   A name given to someone who hasn't learned the truth about inflation yet.

Lender of last resort.   How your children view you.

Letter stock.   Stock so crummy you're legally restrained from selling it.

Leverage.   A way to magnify your losses.

Leveraged buyout.   Using someone else's money to buy the company; also known as betting on the come.

Liabilities.   The main components of your portfolio.

Lien. What you do before you fall.

Limit order. On the buy side, this is something that will keep you out of the stock before the price really goes through the roof.

Limited partnership. Untalented investors who band together to lose money as a group.

Liquid asset. Stock in a beer company.

Liquidation. Beer company stock that went skunky.

Listed security. A stock sinking toward starboard.

Load fund. The word "load" here comes from the concept of loaded dice, and so do the fund's chances for success.

Loan. Something only those who don't need can qualify for.

Locked in. A phrase used at cocktail parties to make the other person think you've made so much off your stocks you couldn't pay the taxes if you sold.

Long. What your face is when the market goes down.

Long-range corporate plan. The directors decide where they'll have lunch tomorrow.

Long-term investment. Any investment made for more than one day.

M

Macroeconomics. The science of mis-reading the economy on a grand scale.

Management. The Marx brothers in three-piece suits.

Manipulation. An overt, rampant prac-tice prior to creation of the SEC, which has reduced the practice to a covert, rampant one.

Margin. Not being given all the rope you want.

Margin call. Where all the rope you were given was too much.

Mark to the market. Keeping your losses current.

Market order. Being in the wrong stock at the right time.

Market risk. Being in the right stock at the wrong time.

Market slump. Being in any stock at any time.

Market value. What your stocks used to have.

Marketable securities. What yours no longer are.

Maturity. Something your bonds will never see.

Merger. The joining together of two bad companies.

Microeconomics. Using supply and demand to explain your stock market misfortunes.

Minority freezeout. Finding out firsthand that might makes right.

Mixed market. A market where all stocks go up except yours.

Modern portfolio theory. An up-to-date way to lose your shirt in the market.

Monetarist. A free-market economist who wants tight government control over the money supply.

Monetary policy. Using the word *policy* to dignify the Fed's madness.

Monetizing the debt. Your spouse leaves town with your checkbook.

Money market fund.   An institution that will pay you an average rate of return for an above-average risk.

Money markets.   Places where people take away your money.

Money supply.   The service you continually offer the market.

Moody's investment grade.   What your best bonds will never qualify for.

Moral obligation bond.   The financial equivalent of believing in the tooth fairy.

Moral suasion.   Further proof that talk is cheap.

Mortgage bonds.   Losing money on someone else's house.

Municipal bonds.   Proof that not only can you not fight City Hall, but you shouldn't invest in it either.

Mutual funds.   A way to get professional assistance in picking bad investments.

Naked option. Losing more than your shirt in the call market.

NASDAQ. A system that provides stock price quotations on every OTC stock under the sun, except the one you're interested in.

National debt. Where the miracle of compound interest comes home to roost.

Negotiable CD. The bank admits up front that if you're smart you won't leave your money with it until maturity.

Net asset value. The true value of a load fund share, which is about 7 to 8 percent under what you'll have to pay for it.

Net income. Another of the many accounting incomes; it really means *not* income

Net worth. The negative number you get when you subtract liabilities from assets.

New account. Fresh meat.

New issues. Something so good your broker never cuts you in on them.

Nifty fifty.   A cute way to describe a collection of fifty dreadful stocks.

No-load fund.   A mutual fund whose management has ways to clip you other than charging a sales commission.

No par stock.   An indication the accountants don't think the stock is worth anything either.

Nominal interest rate.   The bank's way of stating loan rates to disguise how much they're really charging you.

Nominal yield.   What you get on a bond that doesn't earn much.

Noncallable.   A bond so bad that management doesn't want it back.

Nonrecurring earnings.   What earnings for your stocks do all the time.

Not rated.   A bond that's so bad Moody's refuses to look at it.

Notes.   Reminders that debt is risky.

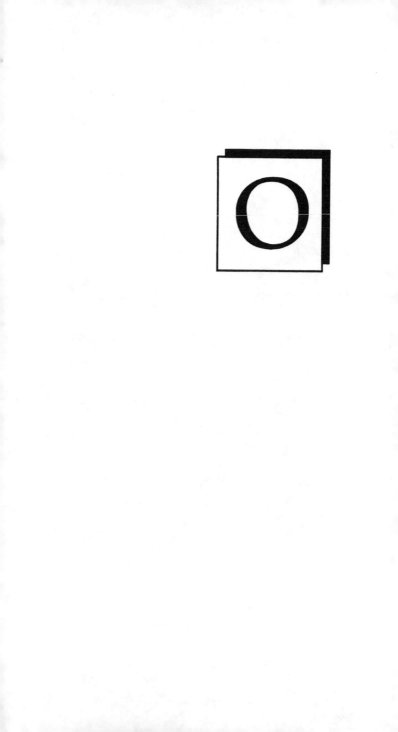

Obscene profits. Something you hear about, but never experience yourself.

Odd lot. Everyone connected with the securities industry.

Odd lot commission. Proof that the small investor is much beloved in the stock market.

Off-balance sheet financing. Refutation of the theory that what you can't see can't hurt you.

Offshort. A mutual fund version of Jaws.

Open-end investment company. A situation where there's no limit to your losses.

Open interest. A rough indication of how many crazies are in the futures market.

Operating lease. Renting cars from a surgeon.

Option. A contract where the other party has a formidable array of painful alternatives that can be inflicted upon you, at will.

Option premium. What you pay the other party to expose yourself to the aforenamed formidable array.

Original issue discount bond. A bond you lost money on from the first moment you bought it.

Out of the money. A horse racing term applied with equal justification to the options market.

Over-the-counter (OTC) market. The financial version of a greasy spoon restaurant.

Overnight position. Long-term commitment by a dealer.

Oversubscribed. An excuse you broker used to explain why you couldn't buy any new issue shares.

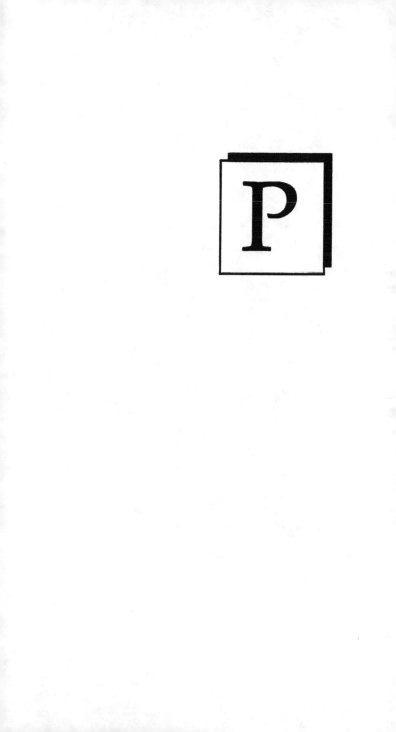

Paper losses.   Your advisor's attempt to shrug off how bad things really are.

Paper profits.   Something you have plenty of until right before your long-term capital gains qualifying date.

Par value.   A meaningless number that is watched closely.

Participating preferred.   A way for preferred stockholders to share in the especially good times that come the common stockholders' way; better known as the "two times nothing equals nothing" feature.

Partnership.   Sharing your losses with others.

Passed dividend.   A football term misapplied; it would be more descriptive to say a punted dividend.

Pass-throughs.   Your home mortgage is sold to Attila the Collector.

Payout ratio.   How much more money you've poured into your stock than you've gotten out.

Pennant.   A baseball term applied to technical analysis to remind you that most stocks have little chance of winning.

Penny stocks.   What your stocks become soon after you buy them.

Pension fund.   What management just raided to finance that new corporate jet.

Perfect markets.   Nothing's absolutely perfect, but this is a good way to console yourself after you fail to beat the market yet one more time.

Performance measurement.   Tallying up how badly you did last year.

Perpetual bond.   A bond where there is no hope of recovering the principal.

Point and figure charting.   Graphically tracking only the big losses.

Portfolio.   A group of securities every bit as attractive as a collection of modern art.

Preemptive right.   Owning first chance to buy more bad stock.

Preferred stock.   A class of stock that is more desirable only in name.

Premium. What you always pay, but never receive.

Present value. A technical term often used to explain why you got shelled in the bond market.

Price-earnings (P/E) ratio. An aid to stock selection that a third of the world's investment advisors say should be low to be favorable, while another third say should be high. The remaining third say it doesn't matter.

Price gap. The unfavorable difference between what you paid for the stock and what you sold it for.

Price inertia. A physics explanation of why your stocks aren't following the rally.

Primary earnings. One of several ways to express stockholders' profit, in the hopes that one of them occasionally will be positive.

Primary market. When even the first graders do better than you.

Prime rate. To quote a major New York bank, "the prime rate is defined to be the rate of interest publicly announced by the bank as its prime rate."

Principal. Often confused with principle, of which there is little on Wall Street.

Private placement. How the *really* good bonds are issued.

Privileged issue. Being killed with kindness.

Pro forma statement. A projection of bad things to come.

Profit and loss statement. A more apt description would be to delete the words "Profit and."

Profit margin. How bad the loss was in percentage terms.

Prospectus. A flyer on some bad mining shares.

Proxy. Giving your vote to a bleached blond.

Prudent man rule. What the trustees of your family's battered trust can prove they followed.

Public offering. Adapting an old Roman sacrificial custom to the stock market.

Pure discount bonds. Finding out that purity is a high price to pay for rate of return.

Put option. A device—taken from the card game Hearts—to pass the stock market equivalent of the queen of spades between two investors.

Pyramiding. Setting yourself up for King Tut's revenge.

Qualified opinion. The auditor's tactful suggestion that the client firm's accountants are incompetent, crooked or both.

Qualitative factor. When your stocks get zapped by something that can't be measured.

Quality of earnings. What your broker talks about when the quantity of earning is low.

Quarterly statement. An interim report on how badly things are going.

Quick ratio. A calculation made hurriedly.

Quotation. The price at which you can never execute your order.

R

Raider. That social, moral and financial degenerate that management just thwarted, whose only redeeming feature was that he would pay you a lot more for your stock than it's worth now.

Rally. Something your stocks and bonds need to do a lot of just to get you back to break-even.

Random walk hypothesis. A simple explanation—that your broker never mentions to you—of why you can't beat Forbes' Dart Fund.

Rate of return. What the other guy always gets more of than you.

Rating agencies. Those folks who downgrade bonds right after you buy them.

Ratio analysis. Dividing a disheartening number by a discouraging number and getting a rosy result.

Real estate investment trust (REIT). An organization that can help you lose money in the real estate market.

Real rate of interest.   The economists' attempt to persuade every one that interest rates aren't as high as they seem.

Recapitalization.   Being run over by the same truck twice.

Receivership.   Another football term applied to finance that, loosely interpreted, means the opposition intercepted and ran it back for the winning touchdown.

Redemption.   The religious concept of hope applied to the bond market.

Redeploying assets.   The finance version of a Pyrrhic victory.

Red herring.   The one shining example of truth in advertising in the securities industry.

Refunding.   Something any reputable department store will do, but your broker will not.

Registered representative.   A brokerage house employee who is licenced to steal.

Registered security.   A stock not approved by the National Rifle Association.

Regulation T. An old football formation that would be about as effective today as the government regulation named after it.

Reinvestment rate. What you could earn on your bond coupons if the bond weren't in default.

Reorganization. A dignified name for bankruptcy.

Repatriating profits. What your company would do with its foreign profits, if it had any.

Replacement cost. What your company assets are worth in an inflationary environment, not forgetting that anything times zero is still zero.

Repurchase agreement (REPO). A security so bad that to sell it you have to agree to buy it back.

Reserves. What your bank didn't have when they were needed most.

Resistence level. What your stock's price just crashed through.

Restructuring. A euphamism for "Well, it didn't work that way, so how about this?"

Retained earnings. Where the dividends you never receive go.

Return on assets. Something your company wouldn't know about.

Return on equity. The financial equivalent of "wait 'til next year."

Return on investment. As Will Rogers once said, what you should really be concerned with is return *of* your investment.

Revenue bonds. A bad way to finance a hamburger shop.

Reverse split. The only way your stock's price will ever rise.

Rights. If you don't exercise or sell them, they turn into wrongs.

Risk. What the other guy gets away with.

Risk-free interest rate. You must be joking!

Risk premium. What you're supposed to receive for risk bearing, but don't.

Rollover. Something your dog can do better than your bond broker.

Round lot. A group of chubby market makers.

Run up. Something only stocks you're shorting do.

S

Safe harbor. Something that boats can find, but money can't.

Sale and lease back. Throwing in the towel and coming back for more, simultaneously.

Scalper. A market maker who learned his trade at Little Big Horn.

Scrip. Future tense of scrap.

Seasonal fluctuation. Your broker's euphemism for a 100 point drop in the Dow.

Seasonal issue. A stock that acts like the Christmas goose.

Seat. Polite synonym for what you lost in the market yesterday.

Secondary distribution. Where the principals bail out of the stock.

Secured loan. What all the other lenders had.

Securities and Exchange Commission (SEC). A federal agency that protects investors by tightly restricting their actions.

Security analyst. The financial counterpart—with even worse accuracy—of a weather forecaster.

Selling climax. A naive expression of hope during a rout.

Serial bonds. Bonds not worth two Wheaties box tops.

Shareholders' equity. A misrepresentation of what the shareholders get.

Shelf rule. A device for helping companies peddle bad securities without interminable delays.

Short sale. Selling something you don't own, which in any other market would get you thrown in jail.

Short term. To vulgarize Professor Keynes, a period of time where we all wish we were dead.

Simple interest. A way for the bank to disguise how much they're really charging us.

Sinking fund. A nautical description of your mutual company.

Small cap stocks. A haberdashery term that should remind you that you can lose your short in the stock market.

Soft market. A place to get hard lumps.

Special situation. After two of these you'll gladly tell your broker not to do you any more favors.

Specialist. A person charged with maintaining a fair and orderly market for a security, unless it's profitable to do otherwise.

Speculation. An investment after its gone bad.

Spin-off. Being thrown into orbit by a callous management.

Split. A gymnastics term describing a painful activity.

Spot market. Being taken to the cleaners, now in pesos.

Spread. Riding two horses at one time in opposite directions.

Stabilization. The quiet that comes after a thirty point drop in your favorite stock.

Standard & Poor's 500. Stocks that are long on pedigree and short on performance.

Statement of changes. An accounting statement that equates asset losses with equity losses.

Statement of retained earnings. A summary of how much management hasn't paid you over the years.

Statistics. A way to tell sophisticated lies.

Steer. A bull with an important part missing.

Stock dividend. What your company pays instead of cash dividends in the belief the two are equivalent.

Stop order. Something you should have put in two weeks ago.

Straddle. An extremely awkward position where you either buy or sell both a put and a call with equally bad striking prices.

Strap. What you find yourself in when you own both a straddle and a call.

Street name.   Owning stocks that are so bad you need an alias.

Striking price.   The price at which someone clobbers you in the options market.

Strip.   Losing your money in the options market without accompanying music.

Subordinated bonds.   Formal acknowledgement that the other guy's bonds are better than yours.

Sunk cost.   Or, as your broker lightheartedly says, "in for a dime, in for a dollar."

Supply side economics.   What you pin your hopes on when demand side economics won't work.

Switching.   A railroad term for being thrown off the main line.

Syndicate.   A sinister but appropriate name for a group of investment bankers.

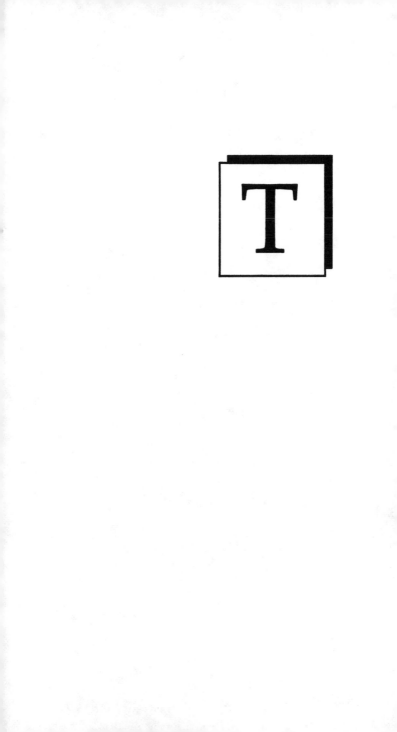

Take-over bid.   Something another company made today on the stock you sold last month.

Tax deduction.   A moment of perfect union between what your accountant believes he can get away with and what the IRS fails to notice.

Tax-exempt bonds.   Bonds whose yields are so bad the government doesn't have the heart to tax them.

Tax refund.   A mythical beast that you've heard of but never seen.

Tax selling.   What you would do at the end of the year with your stock winners to balance off realized capital losses . . . if only you had some winners.

Tax shelter.   Your straw house that the IRS just blew down.

Technical analysis.   A way to lose money for no fundamental reason.

Technical downturn.   A drop in prices that no one can explain.

Technical rally.   All the stocks you just sold start surging.

Tender offer. Your spouse volunteers to burn your worthless stocks.

Term structure. A convenient way to explain why the other guy's bonds always earn higher interest rates.

Theoretical value. A value no one believes.

Thin market. A place to reduce the size of your wallet.

Third market. The financial equivalent of a lesser developed country.

Thrift institution. A group that will pay you less than the current market rate of return on your deposits while simultaneously refusing your home loan application.

Ticker. The Doomsday Machine.

Time value of money. Being killed by compound interest.

Times interest earned. A ratio always less than zero.

Timing. What everyone talks about, but nobody has.

Tip. Advice that is either worthless, illegal or both.

Tombstone. A jocular reminder of how valuable your new issue securities are.

Trader. Someone who takes advantage of ignorant savages.

Trading post. The place where the advantage-taking occurs.

Transactions costs. The trifling amount you pay to buy and sell securities, which also negates, several times over, your trading profits.

Transfer tax. A way for the New York taxing authorities to profit along with the broker who churns your accounts.

Treasury bills (T bills). Securities every bit as safe as the U.S. Government . . . which gives one pause.

Treasury stock. Stock so crummy only the company would buy it.

Trend analysis. Peeking over the brink.

Trustee. A name given to just graduated MBAs who work in bank trust departments.

Turkey. The best investment in your portfolio.

Turnover. What your stomach does while you're watching the ticker tape.

U

Uncertainty. The one thing you can always count on.

Undervalued securities. Everything you just sold.

Unissued stock. Shares that are so bad no one will buy them.

Unseasoned issues. Stocks that the Food and Drug Administration has not approved.

Unsecured bond. The safest portion of your bond portfolio.

Up tick. An event that occurs in an uninterrupted rapid sequence right after you sell.

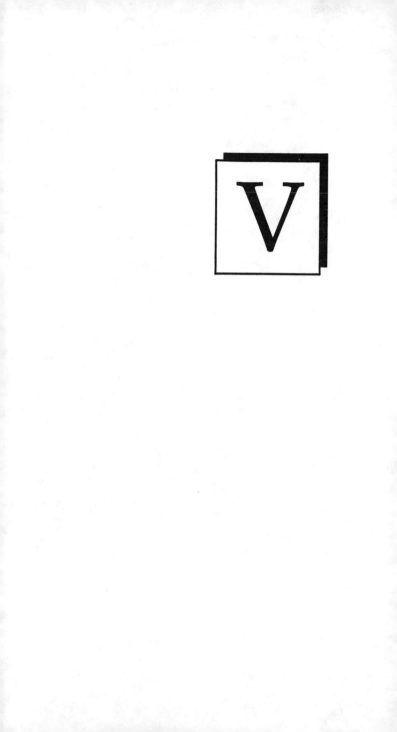

Variable annuity. Being savaged by a life insurance company *before* you die.

Volatile market. A polite way to describe Black Thursday.

Volume. Something analysts talk about when there's nothing more exciting going on.

Voting rights. What the majority stockholders just did you out of.

Wall Street. An expensive place to get mugged.

Wall Street Week. A TV show—run by a man who looks like George Washington and sounds like Henny Youngman—that tells you the newest ways to get mugged.

Warrant. What the sheriff should serve your friend who gave you the hot tip.

Wash sale. Something the IRS never checks on, except in your case.

Wasting assets. Everything you own.

When issued. The answer to the question: When did this stock's price go down?

White knight. Where the stockholders get clobbered by corporate chivalry.

Windows. Since 1929, brokerage offices try not to have any of these above the second story.

Working capital. Something your capital refuses to do.

World Bank. An eleemosynary institution that lends only to countries that can't possibly repay the loan.

WPPSS bonds. A good example of high-quality municipal bonds.

Yankee bonds. Letting George Steinbrenner and Billy Martin manage your investments . . . together.

Yield.   A wrestling term that means "to give up."

Yield curve.   A graph that shows how much your bonds give up over time.

Yield to maturity.   What you would have earned on your bonds had the company not given up.

Zero bonds. A descriptive term for the price of your bonds.